dial it down, LIVE IT UP

8 STEPS TO SIMPLIFY YOUR LIFE

JEFF DAVIDSON

simple truths®
Your Destination For Inspiration
an imprint of Sourcebooks, Inc.

Editing by: Alice Patenaude

Photo Credits:
Cover: Hemera Technologies/Thinkstock; Bozena_Fulawka/Thinkstock
Internal: page i, Hemera Technologies/Thinkstock; page iii, flas100/Thinkstock, FulopZsolt/Thinkstock; page iv, Digital Vision/Thinkstock; page 1, wawritto/Thinkstock, dimdimich/Thinkstock; page 2, Design Pics/Thinkstock; page 4, Vladyslav Starozhylov/Thinkstock; pages 4–5, Andrey Kuzmin/Thinkstock; page 6, KellyISP/Thinkstock; pages 10–11, howellru/iStockphoto; page 12, Elena Elisseeva/Thinkstock; pages 14–15, Mike Powell/Thinkstock; page 17, tonivaver/Thinkstock; page 18, Zoonar/J.Wachala/Thinkstock; page 23, Givaga/Thinkstock; page 24, Vasyl Yakobchuk/Thinkstock; page 26, dterminal/Thinkstock; page 31, phortona/amanaimagesRF/Thinkstock; page 32, Artush/Thinkstock; pages 34–35, jamieroach/Thinkstock; page 37, Purestock/Thinkstock; page 39, AndreaAstes/Thinkstock, Wavebreakmedia Ltd/Thinkstock; page 40, Jupiterimages/Thinkstock; pages 42–43, jegesvarga/Thinkstock; page 44, Kamil Macniak/Thinkstock; page 47, Artem Povarov/Thinkstock; page 48, Ryan McVay/Thinkstock; page 50, rezkrr/Thinkstock; pages 52–53, Ingram Publishing/Thinkstock; page 54, aekikuis/Thinkstock; pages 56–57, Nadezhda1906/Thinkstock; page 58, Wavebreakmedia Ltd/Thinkstock; page 60, thumb/Thinkstock; page 63, monticello/Thinkstock; pages 64–65, Zoonar/S.Heap/Thinkstock; page 66, Jupiterimages/Thinkstock; pages 68–69, Creatas Images/Thinkstock; pages 72–73, Yamtono_Sardi/Thinkstock; page 75, gradisca/Thinkstock; page 77, William Perugini/Thinkstock; pages 78–79, nyaho nayho/amanaimagesRF/Thinkstock; page 80, Catherine Yeulet/Thinkstock; pages 82–83, jordacheir/Thinkstock; pages 86–87, carloscastilla/Thinkstock; page 88, Osuleo/Thinkstock; pages 90–91, Evgeny Sergeev/Thinkstock; page 95, Digital Vision/Thinkstock; pages 96–97, Dorling Kindersley/Thinkstock; pages 98–101, Sashsmir/Thinkstock; page 102, Michael Vigliotti/Shutterstock; page 103, Olga Kleshchenko/Shutterstock; page 104, Artishok/Shutterstock; page 105, Michael Vigliotti/Shutterstock; page 106, Olena Boronchuk/Thinkstock

Published by Simple Truths, an imprint of Sourcebooks, Inc.
P.O. Box 4410, Naperville, Illinois 60567-4410
(630) 961-3900
Fax: (630) 961-2168
www.sourcebooks.com

Printed and bound in the United States of America.
WOZ 10 9 8 7 6 5 4 3 2 1

Contents

Acknowledgments

Mac Anderson, founder of **Simple Truths**, was instrumental in the development of this book, first suggesting the idea to me, helping to select the title, and, through his executive assistant, Darci Bertoncello, shepherding the project through the publishing process.

Alice Patenaude ably served as project and crackerjack copy editor, Lynn Harker as art editor, and Heather Hall as production editor. My student assistants, Casey Peterson and Steven Hinkle, provided critical editing and proofreading.

Thought leaders through the ages on the overall theme of simplicity continue to guide me: Henry David Thoreau, Aldous Huxley, Vance Packard, Eric Hoffer, Thích Nhất Hạnh, Neil Postman, Robert Fritz, and Rachel Remen, among innumerable others.

Emanuel and Shirley Davidson offer eternal inspiration. Peter Hicks, Dianna Booher, John O'Conner, Jeff Stevens, and Martin Horn provide a constant stream of new insights, while Sharon Shelton opens up new worlds of thought and perspective. Valerie Davidson is my constant inspiration.

COMPLEXITY IS A UNIVERSAL NORM

In my travels as a professional speaker, audiences near and far keep bringing up a pervasive issue: the continual need to uncomplicate their personal and professional lives in an era that offers too many choices and too much information. Despite every article written to date, people's lives aren't getting simpler; just the opposite is occurring.

Men and women in virtually every industry and profession today face a bewildering array of "stuff" that competes for their time and attention. By revealing fundamental truths as well as little-known realities on the path to a less encumbered life, *Dial It Down, Live It Up* serves as a handy guide to a life and career of greater grace and ease.

To begin, we need to understand that complexity is a universal norm, while simplicity in your life is an achievable exception.

The next time you're out and about, seek an open field or go to the country, away from human development. What do you see? Trees, bushes, shrubs, wildflowers, grass, birds, bees—all types of growth and life.

> **Abundance is the natural state of earth,
> of nature, and of the universe.**

To profoundly grasp the inherent complexity of life in our universe, visit a rain forest with dense undergrowth that has been undisturbed for centuries. A single rain forest can contain between 10,000 and 1,000,000 species of life not yet documented by human science. A single tree can contain from one to 10,000 uncataloged species. How could such myriad forms of life have developed if nature were inherently plain and simple?

SURROUNDED BY COMPLEXITY

All of us were born in an era when complexity has become the hallmark of our existence. With each passing second, *more information becomes newly available* than you could ingest at typical viewing and reading speed in the next eighty years!

No previous generation on earth has had more items competing for its time and attention. In his entire life, George Washington never spent a second watching CNN *Headline News* or making a Facebook post, and he had no Twitter followers!

> **The infrastructure that holds society in place is based on increasingly sophisticated systems, technology, and complexity.**

COMPLEXITY IS FOR REAL

We've arrived at the point where technology and information come hurtling toward us; we're pummeled by innumerable rules, instructions, and laws that we are expected to know and heed. It's no wonder we feel overwhelmed and exhausted.

Not surprisingly, more people are reassessing how they work and live in order to achieve a simpler, more effective lifestyle that doesn't sacrifice what matters to them. That's what *Dial It Down, Live It Up* is all about.

Be assured, simplicity is within your grasp. To paraphrase Abraham Lincoln, if you are "resolutely determined" to achieve something, you are "half done already."

ON THE PATH TO A SIMPLER EXISTENCE

Seeking a simpler life is not a twenty-first-century phenomenon, nor a new age fad, and it didn't begin in California! The desire for simplicity has been evident for centuries.

In early America, simple living advocates challenged consumerism and materialism. Puritans were known for their religious devotion, hard work, unadorned dress, plain homes, and simple lives. Throughout the 1800s, philosophers and authors, from Henry David Thoreau and Ralph Waldo Emerson to the sharp-tongued, lesser-known John Ruskin, advocated differing forms of simplicity for their inherent virtue.

Today, the term *simplicity* means different things to different people. For some, it is the quest for more control over their time or space, with less to clean or maintain. For others, it's having less stress, fewer bills to pay, or more leisure time. Many associate simplicity with a peaceful state of mind, often linked with spirituality. Your personal quest for simplicity might encompass one or all of these.

If you're in a highly demanding job, with staggering professional and personal responsibilities, take heart: legions of others feel the same as you do.

The challenges in achieving simplicity, while unprecedented, *can be overcome.*

MASTERS CAN READ THE TRAIL

To achieve greater simplicity in your own life, the subtle line between becoming a master and being a novice is knowing how to read the trail beyond the readily apparent. Are you ready for mastery?

Mastery begins with the basic notion that you're the captain of your fate. You're in control. You steer the rudder, pull the lever, flip the switch, call the shots, and have the ability to follow the trail that leads to simplicity.

When you master the elements of simplicity, you don't repeatedly traverse the same undesired trails. You can become like the Bushmen of Namibia, who are so adept at reading footprints that they can tell what a leopard did the day before they started following it.

As you read the following steps to simplicity, keep in mind these perspectives for our increasingly complex world:

Acknowledge the reality of our era. Merely being born guarantees that you will face a never-ending stream of complexity within your home, on the highway, at work, and everywhere in between. Embracing this basic reality is vital to resolution. Sadly, some people won't attain this level of understanding and will blame others, or themselves, for their complex lives. Complexity is no one's "fault."

Convert the question. When facing a challenge, use language that empowers you rather than leaves you in a quandary. Rather than ask "What can I do?" ask yourself "What *will* I do?"

Seek your answer within the problem. Charles Kettering's approach to problem solving remains unsurpassed. He was a founder of the Sloan-Kettering Institute and a brilliant inventor, perfecting the diesel engine, automobile ignition systems, chrome painting, and dozens of other innovations that transformed the auto industry in the 1920s and '30s.

Kettering studied the solutions to problems he or others *had already solved* and reached the conclusion *that solutions lie within the problem.*

He noted that solutions were merely a change in perception, since the solution to the problem existed all along, within the problem itself. A problem solver's role was not to master a problem, but to make it generate its solution.

So, in your pursuit of simplicity, when you encounter a problem, recognize that *your solution likely is right alongside the problem itself.*

Let's take a look at eight steps
to making your life a simpler one.

STEP 1: HANDLING CHOICE OVERLOAD

A typical U.S. supermarket carries at least 38,000 items, twice as many as decades ago. There are so many different products and brands that your choices can seem overwhelming. At work, how do you handle the endless options of vendors, systems, software, products, and service solutions?

While manufacturers seek to differentiate their products and survive in a crowded marketplace, if we focus intently on what we want or need, the net result is more time, effort, and energy.

"You have succeeded in life when all you really want is only what you really need."

—VERNON HOWARD

CHOICE OVERLOAD

Too many choices, as author Alvin Toffler told us more than forty years ago in his landmark book *Future Shock*, inhibit our ability to choose. We now face what he called "future shock," meaning our ability to effectively decide shuts down.

Whether it's athletic shoes, cell phone options, bagels, bottled water, or tennis rackets, too many choices, like too much information, do not serve us.

Simplicity, rather than complexity, should be your product preference among items that are otherwise equal in terms of cost, durability, expected life cycle, and warranty. If one item has dozens of features while another has only a handful (namely the ones you *need*), choose the latter and don't fret about a possible upgrade later.

Learn how to dial down the number of choices to make a wise selection. You've sprung yourself from a complexity trap and handled choice overload.

ℋANDY CHECKLISTS

Creating checklists can also help you avoid choice overload, providing an easy tool for evaluating a potential vendor, product, or service offering. Review everything from a product's design, quality, and features to its cost considerations and whether quantity discounts are available. Ask yourself whether the product will fit within the location you plan to keep it, if there's a guarantee, or if you would need to buy any other items to make it work.

When you have to make a choice, often all you need is a good set of questions to guide you, save you time, maintain peace of mind, and come up smiling!

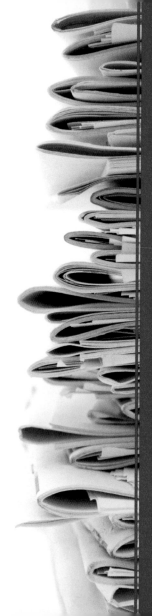

STEP 2: FORSAKING INFORMATION CRUTCHES

A s a result of the daily bombardment of information and choices, we often use information crutches such as backup copies or oversubscription to numerous publications.

While we need to stay abreast of important developments in our own industry or profession and our respective communities, some career professionals oversubscribe and invariably become overwhelmed in an attempt to "stay on top of it all." No one can keep pace with every little thing. You have to decide to devote your attention to issues that merit it. Attempting to take in everything leads to the feeling of drowning in information.

$\mathcal{A}$PPROACHING RAIN BARRELS

So, how can you proceed effectively in the face of constant information overload? Here's an analogy: suppose you're stranded somewhere far from home. You're parched, and miraculously, you encounter a nearly full rain barrel. Would you lift the rain barrel to take a few sips? Even if you're able to lift the barrel (water weighs sixty-two pounds per cubic foot), this would be a difficult way to drink.

What if you had a small cup and could scoop a few ounces of water at a time? If you wanted more, you could refill the cup and continue to quench your thirst.

When you attempt to ingest too much of the daily deluge of information, you're liable to drown in it. You only need to scoop out digestible amounts of information.

Maintain focus on the vital issues, and let the peripheral ones fall by the wayside. Make conscious choices about where you'll give your time and attention.

DATA, DATA EVERYWHERE BUT NOT A THOUGHT TO THINK

Sometimes we collect extensive information to resolve an issue and entirely forget about other ways of reaching the same answer. Depending on the size of your personal or professional network, you're likely to only be three calls away from an expert. You ask one person who refers you to someone else, who either has the answer for you or sends you to the third and ultimate party.

Before collecting volumes of information to resolve an issue, ask yourself: Has someone else tread the same path? Can earlier trailblazers save you oodles of time by sharing their findings and conclusions?

You could also brainstorm your way to a solution. Brainstorming doesn't need to be formal, nor does the size of the group matter; you can even brainstorm with yourself. Pose a question and let the ideas fly. Write down everything you think of, no matter how outlandish. Later, you can go back and delete the totally inane and unworkable.

Some people develop their best ideas while in the shower, rocking in a hammock, or simply humming a tune, often when they weren't even thinking of the issue. This is known as the *eureka effect*.

The answer also might present itself simply with the passage of time. So, if you have a few days to mull over a particular issue, the answer might become clear during that time.

ℬYPASS PROCEDURES

You benefit from any method of bypassing reams of information to arrive at an effective solution. Because today's powerful search engines can answer many of our questions in a matter of seconds, it doesn't make sense to excessively retain hard copies or electronically stored information.

Becoming adept at forsaking information crutches and relying more on your ability to quickly ferret the information you need leads to a greater sense of grace and ease.

"To a man with a hammer, everything looks like a nail... To a man with a computer, everything looks like data."

—NEIL POSTMAN

STEP 3: TAPPING THE POWER OF INTUITION

Typically, to make a work-related decision, career professionals gather all the information they can on a topic. Yet, more data is not always the best approach.

A TALE OF TWO PURCHASES

Let's look at an example. Two groups of executives were given the same task—to make a key equipment purchase. The first group approached the assignment by collecting articles, product descriptions, fact sheets, and expert opinions, and then made their decision.

The second group was asked to choose based upon what they *felt* would represent a wise purchase—to choose based on intuition and instinct.

Weeks after the purchases were made, each group saw the results. Which group do you expect was happier with its decision? The scores

were roughly equal! The group that had chosen based on extensive information and analysis was no more satisfied with their acquisition than the group that chose based on instinct and intuition.

Such results seem to defy all that we've been taught. Choosing based heavily on instinct and intuition, however, is not some hocus-pocus method of making a selection.

CELLULAR LEVEL INTELLIGENCE

All of your intelligence, right down to the cellular level, is brought to bear when you make a decision based on instinct. Regardless of your age, everything you have learned up until *this minute* shapes the process, whether or not you are aware of it.

When he was commanding the troops during Desert Storm in 1991, General Colin Powell used a combination of techniques to arrive at decisions quickly, without information crutches. As the general describes it, when he needed to make a critical decision, such as whether to attack in the morning or later in the day, he would collect about 60 percent of the information he felt was necessary for his decision.

He knew he had to have sufficient data, but he still had to be able to make a quick and effective decision, particularly when time was of the essence. A wrong decision could endanger his troops. So, near the 60 percent mark (and this determination is always an approximation), he relied upon his intuition to complete the analysis and make his decision. His decisions largely proved to be wise choices.

More often than you might surmise, you already have within you enough accumulated "data" to make a sound decision without having to do extensive, additional research.

Your SECOND AND THIRD BRAIN

The value of relying on instinct when making decisions is backed by science. Pioneering studies by physiologists and gastroenterologists indicate there is a "second brain" inside the intestines. Known as the enteric nervous system, "it is independent of and interconnected with the brain in the cranium," says Michael Gershon, MD, chair of the anatomy and cell biology program at Columbia University.

Neurocardiologists also have discovered a "brain in the heart." Composed of more than 40,000 neurons of various types, along with a complex network of neurotransmitters, proteins, and support cells, it acts independently of the head.

According to researcher Robert Cooper, PhD: "This 'heart brain' is as large as many key areas of the thinking brain and sufficiently sophisticated to rate as a brain in its own right." So, with a second brain in your gut and a third in your heart, you've got even more brains than you thought! Cooper observes that "gut instincts are real and warrant listening to."

> **The heart is open to possibilities and actively scans for them, seeking new, intuitive understanding.**

TAPPING THE POWER

To become more adept at tapping into the power of your intuitive choices, write down your "intuitive choice" before making any final decision. When sufficient time has passed, discern the results of your analytical decision. Log the results and compare them to your intuitive choice. Consistently logging choices enables you to track the accuracy of your intuitive choices versus your traditional decision-making processes. You might end up surprising yourself.

As you begin to note how often your intuitive choices prove to be good ones, you'll rely on your intuition more easily and more often.

$\mathscr{A}$ MATTER OF TRUST

Complexity takes no holidays. While you can't always forgo research in making decisions, you can only absorb a fraction of the information you encounter every day. Fortunately, you don't have to undertake exhaustive research on every single issue that requires a decision. *Trust your instincts!* They will serve you well.

Often, the first notion that comes into your head about a situation is the right one, and you spend time thereafter confirming what you already sensed at the outset.

STEP 4:
DETERMINING WHAT TO TOSS
VERSUS WHAT TO RETAIN

C hances are that you're holding on to too much when it comes to media, gifts, cards, documents, books, guides, magazines, and even outdated equipment.

Why do we find ourselves hanging on to so much? Among many reasons is the fear that if we toss something, the *next* day we'll need it! Or that if we have the space, there's no harm in retaining items we don't use or need. Yet, the more you hang on to, the more you have to manage and, invariably, the more restricted you feel.

"Our life is frittered away by detail.
Simplify, simplify."

—HENRY DAVID THOREAU

FREE AT LAST

Rachel Remen, author of *My Grandfather's Blessings*, tells a poignant story: As a young girl, Rachel's house was ransacked. Her mother had saved, but never worn, some expensive silk stockings. The thief made off with these.

Thereafter, Rachel decided she would use everything she owned. She realized that *having* and *experiencing* are two different phenomena and felt the most free when her possessions were few.

Think back to your days as a student or when you moved into your first home as a young adult. In comparison with today, you probably didn't have anywhere near the number of possessions. Yet, it's likely you felt freer then than you do now. Too many possessions tend to weigh us down.

**If you want to live it up, dial down
the number of items you retain.**

$\mathcal{P}$RACTICE SAFE TOSSING

The following ideas will help you when it comes to tossing what you don't need:

1. ***The Five Times Review***—If you can't determine whether to retain an item or not, review it once a day over five days. At any time during any one of the reviews, if you feel the urge to toss or recycle the item, do so. At the end of five reviews, if you haven't felt the urge to remove the item, then feel free to retain it. On some subconscious level, you have told yourself "this is not the time to part with this item."

2. ***The Cube Test***—If the item(s) you're considering for retention or tossing fit comfortably into a 3x3x3-foot cube (roughly the space under a four-person card table), feel free to retain it. It's likely that you have this space in your home.

3. ***The One-Year Rule***—When you're in a quandary about retaining items, box and store them in an attic, garage, or other area where they will be dry, safe, and secure. Mark the box with

the original storage date. One year later, review the contents of the box. It now might be easier to toss the items. Alternatively, you might decide that the items merit retention. If so, simply close up the box and keep them for another year.

The more items you can safely toss or recycle the better. You'll have more space, a greater feeling of freedom, and potentially more energy.

STEP 5:
SIMPLICITY AND THE
REPLACEMENT PRINCIPLE

When my daughter was in grammar school, her collection of DVD movies had grown to twenty-four. I happened to acquire a DVD case that could hold twenty-four DVDs, including the plastic covers. I made a deal with her: rather than have the DVD collection grow beyond twenty-four and become unmanageable—like some of her other collections—I offered to buy her a new DVD of her choice that same day if she would replace another DVD already in her collection.

She was happy to do so. She had outgrown some of her movies and gladly parted with one for the opportunity to receive a new one. She maintained twenty-four DVDs and then, as new ones arrived, she decided which older ones she would remove.

This replacement principle allows your home or workplace to remain uncluttered, because for each item you add, you remove one. This approach worked so well, I began sharing it with my audiences at conferences and conventions.

"First we form habits, then they form us."

—ROB GILBERT

$\mathcal{G}$OT SHOES?

Some people have too many items in their closets. Whatever the collection, whether it's shoes, coats, or books, many items can safely be removed—you've outgrown them, they're obsolete, they've lost meaning for you, or you're ready to make a change.

The following comparisons are some ways to use the replacement principle so your home or workplace doesn't become cluttered with items you haven't used or enjoyed in years.

Suppose you have old equipment in your closets and storage bins.
Replacement Principle: When you buy new equipment, you donate older, less efficient equipment to a charity and receive a tax deduction.

You've collected books since college and now have overflowing shelves with no hope of reading most of what you've collected.
Replacement Principle: You retain only books of continuing or sentimental value. Scan or copy the key pages of a book from which you want to retain information and then donate the book.

Your CD collection spans many shelves and is completely covered with dust.
Replacement Principle: Sell or donate your CD collection after downloading every song you want for instant play on your smartphone, iPod, or other player.

KEEPING IT MANAGEABLE

You've likely heard of the 80/20 rule—80 percent of the results or value comes from 20 percent of the actions or number of items. This rule applies to your collections as well! For example, if you're a coin collector, 20 percent of your coins likely represent 80 percent or more of the total value of your collection. If you traded the 80 percent for one valuable coin, your collection would have the same value and would fit in one fifth of the space; the same is true for other types of collections.

You don't necessarily have to trade in the bottom 80 percent; you might opt to give them away. Perhaps you have a younger person in mind who would appreciate the jump-start on his or her collection. Or you can donate part of your collection to a worthy cause.

> **When you can identify a recipient for your donation,
> it is easier to reduce the size of your collection.**

When charitable organizations give you a receipt, you gain a tax deduction. So, you benefit in many ways: more space, more manageability, greater enjoyment, the satisfaction of knowing you've helped others, and reduced income taxes. What a deal!

STEP 6:
THE REVENGE EFFECT AND THE
DANGERS OF OVERSIMPLIFYING

In his book *Why Things Bite Back*, Edward Tenner observed a phenomenon he dubbed *the revenge effect*: "The Revenge Effect is the curious way the world has of getting even, defeating our best efforts to speed it up and otherwise improve it." Freeways and beltways around cities, intended to speed travel, lead to suburbs and developments near exits, so commuting times climb.

Computers and printers make it easy to copy and print files, so you copy and print many more files, filling your supposedly *paperless* office.

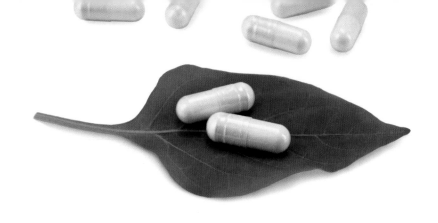

Nearly every breakthrough comes with its own set of pitfalls and drawbacks.

In the early twentieth century, miracle drugs such as antibiotics were widely dispensed to eliminate a host of ancient maladies. Instead, advancing generations of drug-resistant microbes now render antibiotics far short of miracle cures.

STEM THE TIDE

Make your own rules when it comes to adopting technology. For example, determine if you really need the latest model smartphone or tablet. When you view each new technological tool as both beneficial and detrimental, you're better able to keep things simpler. Maybe your current device doesn't do everything newer models do, but if it does what you want—simply—that's all you need.

"A problem well stated is
a problem half solved."

—CHARLES KETTERING

OVERSIMPLIFYING THAT LEADS TO COMPLEXITY

No one is immune to the revenge effect. For example, a celebrated "simplicity guru" apparently downsized her wardrobe to the point where she had two pairs of slacks, two blazers, six turtlenecks, two skirts, and five T-shirts. If you do not have to show up to work five days a week in a professional wardrobe, go ahead and strip your closet.

For most people, reducing a wardrobe to a subsistence level might yield a temporary experience of simplicity. At first, you'll feel good when you look in your closet and see the few clothes you enjoy wearing.

When an item gets torn, another is in the laundry, and you need to leave the house for a social commitment, you'll find that paring down your clothes beyond a sensible level is not an act of simplicity, but an emergency waiting to happen.

$\mathcal{M}$AINTAIN STANDARDS

Some preach that the road to simplicity is to do less: for example, to not make your bed each morning. That's fine if no one ever sees your bedroom. For most people, making the bed is an initiation to the day.

Leaving things undone does not represent simplicity, nor does forsaking cleanliness, order, and decorum. Shortchanging basic tasks in the hopes of saving a few minutes offers a false progression toward simplicity.

Don't follow the gurus to absurdity. If you become a hermit, alienated from the world, saving a few seconds and a few pennies can lead to a boring, shallow existence.

Don't let your quest for simplicity take on zealous, comical, or tragic dimensions!

Pare down your excess items, but do not pare down so much that you reinvite complexity into your life at a future date.

"When people are free to do as they please, they usually imitate each other."

—ERIC HOFFER

STEP 7: ACHIEVING COMPLETIONS IN EVERYDAY LIFE

One of the most effective ways to continually achieve simplicity is by seeking completions of the tasks we begin—a process championed by Robert Fritz in his seminal book *The Path of Least Resistance*.

COMPLETIONS ALL DAY LONG

Each of us already has all the essential elements we need to become masters of completions. From clearing your desk at the end of the workday to cooling down after a workout on the treadmill, each of us achieves a variety of large and small completions each day, whether or not we acknowledge them.

$\mathcal{A}$ PAYOFF EACH TIME

You can even give yourself a completion merely for your thoughts, not only for finished tasks. Perhaps you worked through a troubling issue and came to a resolution. That too is a completion, and the act of acknowledging any completion gives you *more energy, focus, and direction for what comes next.* This is a wonderful gift to give yourself!

When I speak at conferences and conventions, I ask audience members about the biggest completion of their lives. Invariably, someone says "when I got married" or "when I graduated college" or "the arrival of my first child."

The biggest completion of your life, however, is not any of these things, but rather the acknowledgment that *everything up to this minute is a completion of what you have started.*

Whether things went well, or not so well, everything that got you here, all the struggles and triumphs, add up to where you are now. So, acknowledge yourself for having made it this far in your life.

Even if things haven't gone so well, from this moment on is a new beginning. Decide what you want to do next, and don't be surprised if you feel invigorated.

CLEAN AND ENERGIZING

Completions are energizing because they offer a clean end to activities and pave the way for what's next. The most joyful and productive people you know likely have developed the habit of achieving one completion after another, even if they don't call it that. They silently but continually praise themselves for their efforts and are ready to move on to other challenges.

To an outside observer, it might look as if these individuals barely have a moment between what came before and what comes next, but for those who offer themselves silent self-acknowledgment, that demarcation line is enormous.

Completion seekers are not obsessive. They don't seek completions just for their own sake. Beating the clock, obsessive behavior, overachieving, and workaholism are not synonymous with achieving completions. Rather, when you achieve a completion, it provides an effective way to treat your mind and emotions to temporary energy breaks.

Completions can include a variety of everyday tasks, from emptying the trash and making your bed, to balancing your checkbook after every transaction or changing the oil in your car every 3,000 miles.

CONVERTING INCOMPLETIONS INTO COMPLETIONS

In contrast, is your life filled with incompletions? Are any of these examples familiar: accumulating old receipts in your wallet or purse, launching into reading a new book before finishing another, letting old newspapers and magazines pile up, or rushing around to buy gifts the day before a holiday?

If you're guilty of two or more of the above, don't fret. Seek positive completions joyfully, not obsessively. This life-enhancing habit will give you power and energy.

"The miracle is not to walk on water. The miracle is to walk on the green earth in the present moment, to appreciate peace and beauty that are available now... It is not a matter of faith; it is a matter of practice. We need only to find ways to bring our body and mind back to the present moment so we can touch what is refreshing, healing, and wondrous."

—THÍCH NHẤT HANH

STEP 8:
MANAGING THE BEFOREHAND, HANDLING THE UNEXPECTED

Managing the beforehand" means preparing for something in advance. For example, you buy a turkey in advance of a holiday to prepare for the dinner you'll be having. That seems obvious enough. However, managing the beforehand can be used in all aspects of both your professional and personal life to give you a sense of control you might not otherwise experience.

"I'd do anything for a good body except exercise and eat right."

—STEVE MARTIN

PREPARATION THAT COUNTS

Suppose you're heading to a conference the following week. You view a list of exhibitors and conference participants online and you want to make contact with a variety of individuals at this event. To manage the beforehand, you prepare a contact roster including the name, phone number, email, and postal address of each individual.

When you're on-site and can make face-to-face contact, the follow-up is much easier because you've already managed the beforehand.

NOT EMBRACED BY THE MASSES

Most people, and too many organizations and governmental agencies, deal with the *aftermath* of what occurs. For example, if an old bridge collapses, only then does the city highway commission engage in the necessary repair work to keep the road open. Wouldn't it have been more beneficial and less costly to engage in preventive maintenance?

> **Only a small fraction of the population engages in managing the beforehand.**

On a personal level, dealing with the aftermath shows up in a variety of ways. For example, creating clutter because you don't know where to put things is dealing with the aftermath of living in a material society. Managing the beforehand involves allocating space in advance of the arrival of new information or items in your personal or professional life.

Returning home from a meeting with mounds of new publications and reports represents dealing with the aftermath of attending the meeting. Returning home from a meeting with a lean, highly potent file of key ideas represents managing the beforehand—you pare down the pile long before leaving the meeting.

"If you think getting organized is time-consuming, try disorganization."

—JEFF DAVIDSON, *BREATHING SPACE*

AFTERMATH OR BEFOREHAND: YOUR CHOICE

Here are some contrasts between dealing with the aftermath versus managing the beforehand:

Aftermath: Leaving for work in the morning in a mad rush, forgetting things, and feeling stressed when starting your day.

Managing the beforehand: Leaving with grace and ease because you already assembled everything by the door or in your car the night before.

Aftermath: Figuring out how you're going to pay for your child's higher education when you have no savings and he or she is now in high school.

Managing the beforehand: Starting a fund fifteen years in advance that has grown large enough to pay for college and even graduate school!

Aftermath: Panicking when a key employee calls in sick and no one else is prepared to handle the job.

Managing the beforehand: Cross-training your staff members so they can fill in on short notice or having a temp agency on speed dial!

$\mathcal{M}$ORE WORK UP-FRONT, GREATER OVERALL PAYOFF

Why do we wait for the aftermath when we know that completing tasks in advance of dire need reduces complexity? Perhaps it is human nature. Managing the beforehand means extra work at the outset, though far less work than dealing with the aftermath. Ultimately, managing the beforehand requires less time and energy overall and leads to greater achievement and peace of mind!

Managing the beforehand equals dialing it down, thus you can live it up.

Managing the beforehand represents the culmination of the eight steps to a simpler life: when you handle choice overload, summon the strength to forsake information crutches, and rely on your own intuition, you're well on the path. Once you firmly grasp what to toss versus what to retain and adopt the replacement principle to manage the spaces and places in your life, benefits abound.

When you seek completions throughout the day and actively manage the beforehand, you'll be better able to handle the unexpected, roll with the punches, capitalize on emerging opportunities, and feel more satisfied more of the time!

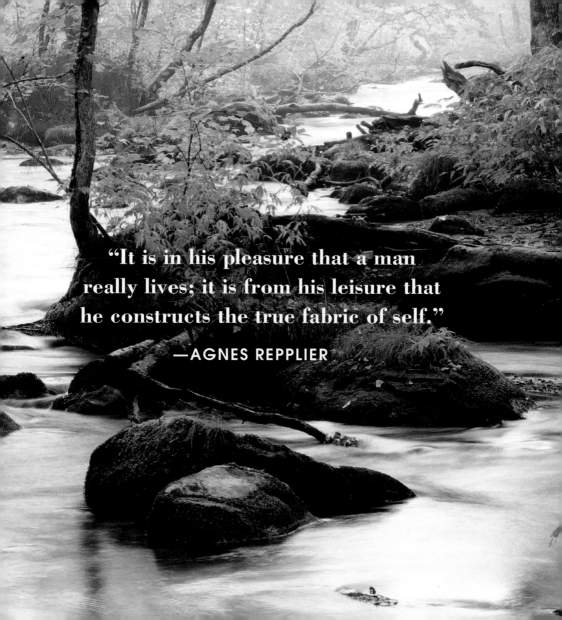

"It is in his pleasure that a man really lives; it is from his leisure that he constructs the true fabric of self."

—AGNES REPPLIER

MOMENTS OF TRUTH

As you practice the eight steps, you will begin to have a sense of breathing space and a greater sense of control. You can step back and take a breath when you want or need to.

Several indicators, what you might call moments of truth, let you know you are on the path to a freer, saner life and that your "dial it down" activities have resulted in your ability to live it up.

For openers, you awake naturally each morning without an alarm clock and have time for reflection. You are able to contemplate what you want to do, who you'll be meeting, and what is expected of you—a more palatable way to start the day than feeling as if you are in a major rush. Start the day hectic, and the whole day might stay that way.

Here's a key moment of truth: you have the ability to leave the workplace on time and become engrossed with your next activity rather than thinking about work. Perhaps you're going straight home, meeting a friend, or attending an event. Finishing work at a reasonable hour, at least a couple times a week, is something we can all achieve.

"This is the time to remember 'cause it will not last forever. These are the days to hold on to 'cause we won't, although we'll want to."

—BILLY JOEL, "THIS IS THE TIME"

THE POSSIBILITIES

Here are other possible moments of truth: You play with your child for hours on a Saturday afternoon with little or no concern about the time, in contrast to past Saturdays, which were filled with activities, many of which you found entirely unrewarding.

Dialing down some activities can also help you to live it up by allowing you more time to do the things you WANT to do:

- Engaging in a hobby with renewed enthusiasm.

- Making new friends who open up new vistas and allow you to experience the world in different ways.

- Volunteering for a charitable activity that interests you. When you devote your time to a cause, it's as if you're telling your subconscious "I'm prosperous enough in my life that I can be of service to others."

- Achieving a weight-loss goal. Most people gain a pound a year following high school. If you set a realistic goal, such as losing one to three pounds a month, you could be twelve to thirty-six pounds lighter within a year.

- Taking naps throughout the week and feeling good about it. Men reportedly can take naps during the day more easily than women. If you're a woman, however, don't let such findings thwart your quest to take an eighteen- or twenty-minute snooze when you have the opportunity. When you awake, you'll feel like a different person.

- Viewing sunrises and sunsets.

- Frequenting some of the area's best parks, and taking time to connect with nature by walking trails, feeding ducks, or rustling through the leaves.

- Increasing your savings or retirement accounts. Start now, regardless of your age. Putting away a little each week, you might surprise yourself as to how much you can accumulate. You can be among that tiny group within the population that actually achieves financial security.

"If you're too busy to enjoy your life, you're too busy."

—JEFF DAVIDSON, *BREATHING SPACE*

LIVING IT UP
IN LITTLE WAYS

What would your life be like if you had the ability to dial it down and live it up, all while tackling problems and challenges as they arise? If you had the space and freedom to engage in innovative thinking? If you had a sense of control and ease about each day?

Whether you work at home or at a traditional workplace, if you follow the eight steps to dialing it down and living it up, you'll start each day with grace and ease.

"Whatever you want to do, do it now.
There are only so many tomorrows."

—MICHAEL LANDON

HERE IS MY VISION FOR YOU

You are able to focus on the most important issues facing your organization, your department, your job, and/or your career. You stay focused most of the time. You are able to handle the day's mail upon its arrival. You're adept at keeping piles from forming. You handle phone calls in a prompt and effective manner. You consistently enjoy a leisurely lunch.

Most days, you depart from the workplace at a reasonable hour and feel good about what you accomplished that day. You take time to enjoy being with friends and relatives, as well as staying in shape and at your desired weight. You have time to participate in hobbies and other leisure activities. You devote time to civic, social, or charitable organizations or any cause you deem worthy.

You identify and attain the resources you need to make your domestic life a pleasure—the right hired help, cleaning services, delivery services, and repair services.

The grace and ease of each day extends to your finances. You file your quarterly and annual income taxes on time and easily pay the monthly mortgage or rent. You have sufficient and up-to-date health, life, disability, and auto insurance.

Beyond all of the above, and best of all, you're able to drop back at any time, take a long, deep breath, collect your thoughts, and renew your spirit.

ACTION SUMMARY

COMPLEXITY IS A UNIVERSAL NORM

- Complexity is a universal norm, but simplicity in your life is an achievable exception.

- Achieving simplicity means having an effective lifestyle without sacrificing what is vital to you.

- Simplicity is within your grasp, and if you are *determined* to have it, you are already halfway to your goal.

ON THE PATH TO A SIMPLER EXISTENCE

- Achieving greater simplicity is possible by knowing how to read the trail beyond the readily apparent.

- Merely being born means you'll face a never-ending stream of complexity.

- When beset by complexity, rather than ask "What *can* I do?" ask yourself "What *will* I do?"

- Look for the answer to complex issues right beside the problem.

STEP 1: HANDLING CHOICE OVERLOAD

- To dial down the number of choices you face to make a wise selection, reduce the options to a manageable number.

- Create checklists to remind you of important factors when making decisions.

STEP 2: FORSAKING INFORMATION CRUTCHES

- Decide which items or issues merit your attention.

- Don't forsake alternative ways of getting an answer: any method to bypass collecting reams of information to arrive at an effective solution is to your benefit.

STEP 3: TAPPING THE POWER OF INTUITION

- All of your intelligence is brought to bear when you make a decision based on instinct or intuition, so don't ignore it.

- Begin to note how often your intuitive choices prove to be good ones and you'll rely on your intuition more easily and often.

STEP 4: DETERMINING WHAT TO TOSS VERSUS WHAT TO RETAIN

- The more you hang on to, the more you have to manage and, invariably, the more restricted you feel, so lighten your load.

- Use everything you own.

- Employ the *five times review*, the *cube test*, and the *one-year rule* to evaluate what to retain.

STEP 5: SIMPLICITY AND THE REPLACEMENT PRINCIPLE

- Replace the outdated with the updated for whatever type of collections you maintain.

- Apply the 80/20 rule to your collections: 20 percent of your holdings likely represent 80 percent of the value.

- To more easily pare down your collections, identify a donation recipient.

STEP 6: THE REVENGE EFFECT AND THE DANGERS OF OVERSIMPLIFYING

- To reduce the chance of experiencing the revenge effect related to technology use, make your own rules and determine if you really need the latest model.

- Avoid paring down below reasonable levels, which reintroduces complexity into your life.

STEP 7: ACHIEVING COMPLETIONS IN EVERYDAY LIFE

- Acknowledge your completions, large and small, to gain a mental and emotional break from what just transpired, and to be better prepared for what comes next.

- Realize that even if things haven't gone well, your experience from this moment on represents a new beginning.

STEP 8: MANAGING THE BEFOREHAND, HANDLING THE UNEXPECTED

- Manage the beforehand by preparing for known events and activities in advance.

- Recognize that managing the beforehand might require more work at the outset, though far less work than dealing with *the aftermath* when you don't take steps in advance.

MOMENTS OF TRUTH

- Moments of truth indicate that you're on the path to a freer, saner life and that your "dial it down" activities have resulted in your ability to live it up.

- A key moment of truth occurs when you have the ability to leave the workplace on time and become engrossed with your next activity rather than with thoughts of work.

LIVING IT UP IN LITTLE WAYS

- Simplicity: You stay focused more of the time.

- Simplicity: You're able to drop back at any time, take a long, deep breath, collect your thoughts, and renew your spirit.

ABOUT THE AUTHOR

Jeff Davidson holds the registered trademark as the Work-Life Balance Expert®. Jeff is the leading personal brand in speaking, writing, and reflecting on work-life balance issues, and he has a passion for speaking to organizations that want to help their employees make rapid progress in this arena. He has spoken to Fortune 100 companies such as IBM, Cardinal Health Group, Lockheed, American Express, Worthington Steel, America Online, Wells Fargo, and Westinghouse, and to the Research Triangle Institute, National Office Furniture, DSM Pharmaceuticals, Novo Nordisk, Swissotel, Re/Max, Experient, and Lufthansa, among five hundred others.

Jeff is the author of *Simpler Living*, *Breathing Space*, *The 60 Second Organizer*, *The 60 Second Self-Starter*, and *The 10-Minute Guide: Stress Management*, as well as twenty-four iPhone apps in his "Work-Life Guide" series on iTunes. Jeff's books have been published in eighteen languages, including Arabic, Chinese, Japanese, Malay, Turkish, and Russian; have been featured in sixty-eight of the top seventy-five American newspapers; and have been promoted in *TIME* magazine and the *Wall Street Journal*.

Jeff has been interviewed nineteen times by publications, including the *Washington Post*, *Los Angeles Times*, *Chicago Tribune*, *Christian Science Monitor*, *New York Times*, and *USA Today*. He currently is a columnist for sixteen publications, among them *Accounting Web*, *Association News*, *Human Resources IQ*, *Inside Business*, *Practical Lawyer*, and *Real Estate Professional*. Jeff also is an advisory board member for *The Organized Executive*, a monthly publication of Columbia Books, Washington, DC. In 2002, he was cited by *Sharing Ideas* magazine in its annual roundup of "consummate speakers."

Learn more about Jeff at www.BreathingSpace.com.